Obvious symmetry soon wearies the eye, stultifies imagination,
closes the episode before it begins.
— Frank Lloyd Wright, An Autobiography, 1932: 303

*The good building is not one that hurts the land-
scape, but one which makes the landscape more
beautiful than it was before that building was built.*
— Frank Lloyd Wright, To Marin County, 1957

FRANK LLOYD WRIGHT'S NAKOMA CLUBHOUSE & SCULPTURES

A HISTORIC PERSPECTIVE

A WRIGHT STUDY

DOUGLAS M. STEINER

Published by Milbourn Publishing Co.,
Edmonds, Washington.

Printed in the United States of America by Gorham Printing,
Centralia, Washington.

Acknowledgments: I would like to thank Caleb Olsen, General Manager at the Nakoma Golf Resort, and the Nakoma Golf Resort, who without their assistance, this book, like the original clubhouse, would not have come to pass. A special thanks to Arnold Roy and John Rattenbury at the Taliesin Architects, Tom Waddell, Oskar Muñoz, Margo Stipe and Doug Volker at Taliesin and Taliesin West for their assistance and support. Mark Hertzberg for his diligent persistence to detail and a push toward excellence. Rebekah Beyer for her editing assistance and suggestions. My adult children who have always encouraged and supported my interest in Frank Lloyd Wright. And most importantly my wife and best friend Christine, who over the past few decades has willingly followed me all over the country in my quest for all things Wright, always encouraging and supportive.

Quotations by Frank Lloyd Wright, courtesy of The Frank Lloyd Wright Foundation.

Design and layout by Douglas M. Steiner.

Endpages: Wigwam Dining Room American Indian Frieze, designed by Frank Lloyd Wright, 1923, adaptation by the author, 2013.

First Edition
Second Printing, 2016
Copyright © 2013 Douglas M. Steiner
All rights reserved.

ISBN: 978-0-615-93547-8

98 Illustrations.

For more information about the
Nakoma Golf Resort.

For more information about
Frank Lloyd Wright.

TABLE OF CONTENTS

The song, the masterpiece, the edifice are a warm outpouring of the heart of man, — human delight in life triumphant: we glimpse the infinite. That glimpse or vision is what makes art a matter of inner experience, — therefore sacred, and no less but rather more individual in this age, I assure you, than ever before.
— Frank Lloyd Wright, Two Lectures on Architecture, 1931: 59

INTRODUCTION

Frank Lloyd Wright's work never ceases to amaze and inspire me, even 53 years past his death. In October 2012, my wife and I had the opportunity to visit the Nakoma Golf Resort, located northwest of Reno, on the northern end of the Sierra-Nevada Mountain Range in California. One year earlier, my nephew Caleb Olsen, Golf Pro and General Manager at Nakoma, called, *"You will never guess where I'm working."*

As we turned onto Bear Run Drive I had to smile. Very clever of the Taliesin Architects. Fallingwater, one of Wright's most famous homes, is built over a stream called Bear Run. Another street is named Fallingwater. My first surprise was to glimpse what I had only visualized from Wright's illustrations created nearly 90 years earlier. Just to the right of the drive were massive statues, placed in a pond, the closest I have seen to how Wright had originally envisioned them. My wife told me to settle down.

Wright's original drawings for the Nakoma and Nakomis statues, known as the "Nakoma Memorial Gateway," originally placed them in two separate pools. The upper pool, "Nakomis Plateau," included the 18-foot rectangular chieftain Nakomis. The lower pool, "Nakoma Basin," included the 16-foot circular Nakoma.[1] In deference to the full sized SC Johnson Headquarters' 1976 statues, these were created at ninety percent of the original height: 16 and 11 1/2 feet respectively.

Like the design for the Nakoma clubhouse, there are other examples of Wright's appreciation of the American Indian heritage. As early as 1895, he commissioned Orlando Giannini to paint American Indian murals in his Oak Park home. John Lloyd Wright, his son, wrote, *"'Skinny' Giannini from Italy painted American Indians in brilliant colors on the walls of Papa's bedroom... Papa liked Indians!"*[2] *(page 27).*

Although Wright originally designed the Nakoma and Nakomis to be set in separate pools, neither the Garners nor the Taliesin Architects can be faulted for placing them in the same pool. They truly form a "gateway" to the Nakoma clubhouse.

The male Nakomis (above) stands 16 feet tall. The female Nakoma (left) stand 11 1/2 feet tall.

Frank Lloyd Wright at 56, 1923. This portrait was taken around the time Wright designed the Nakoma Clubhouse.

Wright at 57, circa 1924. Frank Lloyd Wright working at his drafting table, Taliesin, Spring Green, Wisconsin. Photographed around the time Wright designed the Nakoma and Nakomis sculptures.

Frank Lloyd Wright at 28, 1895. A self-portrait. "No 'picture-taker' could satisfy him. So he rigged up his camera with a long rubber tube, and at the right moment, squeezed the bulb! It was the year 1895." John Lloyd Wright.[3]

FRANK LLOYD WRIGHT

*O*ne of our great redwoods has fallen and left a space we cannot fill by any quick plantation of lesser trees... By general agreement today, he counts as one of the greatest creative artists the nineteenth century brought forth in any field... It took three centuries to grow this man, and it may take an even longer time to plumb the depths of his genius... Lewis Mumford, 1960.[4]

Frank Lloyd Wright was born on June 8, 1867 and died on April 9, 1959. He was an architect, but when given the opportunity, he also designed the interior furnishings and fabrics for his clients. He was a prolific writer, authoring numerous books, countless articles and pamphlets. He was a lecturer and educator, forming his own architectural school called the Taliesin Fellowship. He designed over 1,000 structures, half of which were completed.

His masterpieces are innumerable. The Winslow Residence (1894), his first independent commission, was a step in the development of the Prairie Style. The Susan Dana Residence (1902) has approximately 450 exquisite art glass windows and doors. In 2002, a Wright-designed Dana House lamp sold for nearly two million dollars.

The Architectural Record magazine named the Robie House (1906) one of the most important homes ever built in America. Midway Gardens (1913) and the Imperial Hotel (1915), both demolished, are a tribute to Wright's genius. Hundreds of thousands of tourists visit Wright's own homes every year, including his home and studio in Oak Park, Taliesin near Spring Green and Taliesin West in Scottsdale.

Fallingwater (1935) has been considered the greatest residence ever designed. Ken Burns described the SC Johnson headquarters' Great Workroom (1936) as the greatest room in the United States today. His architecture changed the nation. Simon and Garfunkel even immortalized him in song.

Touring a Wright home or a unique building like the Nakoma clubhouse is like walking through a three dimensional piece of artwork. It surrounds you. It arouses your senses. It touches your soul. The merging of interior and exterior spaces is remarkable. Like other creative and artistic geniuses such as Picasso and Dylan, Wright constantly evolved. He moved from one period to the next, like designing the Moore Residence, Oak Park (1895), then never another in that style.

Wright was recognized in 1991 by the American Institute of Architects as "the greatest American architect of all time."

The U.S. Postal Service commemorated Wright and his work in 1966, Fallingwater in 1982, Robie House in 1998 and the Solomon Guggenheim Museum in 2005.

Solomon R. Guggenheim Museum, New York, 1959.

Robie House, circa 1926.

Original Drawing for the Nakoma Clubhouse,
Frank Lloyd Wright, 1923

Gravity heat, first used in 1915 in the Imperial Hotel in Tokyo,
was planned for the Nakoma Country Club but that Indianesque
affair stayed in the form of a beautiful plan.
— Frank Lloyd Wright, A Testament, 1957: 152

1923: NAKOMA CLUBHOUSE

Madison, Wisconsin, was as close to what Wright would call a home town. In 1878 when he was 11 years old his family settled in Madison. He lived there until 1887 when he moved to Oak Park. One of his earliest projects was remodeling Rocky Roost (1893), a cottage on Lake Mendota, owned by his boyhood friend Robert Lamp. That same year he designed the Lake Mendota and the Lake Monona Boathouses. Ten years later, in 1903, Robert Lamp called on Wright to design a home for him in Madison. Wright also designed the Gilmore Residence in 1908.

Near the turn of the century, Madison experienced remarkable growth. To meet the ever increasing housing demands, farms were platted for subdivisions, including Wingra Park in the early 1890's, University Heights in 1893, Oakland Heights and Randall Park in 1896. By 1910, West Lawn, Highland Park and Edgewood Park were included. At first, home sales were slow due to insufficient transportation. But as automobile ownership increased, so did the sales of outlying lots.

The first lots in the Nakoma subdivision became available in 1915 for $325 to $700. Nakoma is a Chippewa word which means *"I do as I promise"* or *"I keep my word."* A drive through the neighborhood would reveal streets named Chippewa, Hiawatha, Cherokee, Seneca, Yuma, Council Crest and, of course, Nakoma. As sales increased, the Nakoma Country Club was established on land adjacent to the subdivision, nestled on the shore of Lake Wingra. For inspiration and design ideas for their clubhouse, some members may have visited the River Forest Golf Club in Illinois, designed by Frank Lloyd Wright in 1898.

During 1923, while Frank Lloyd Wright was at Taliesin in Spring Green, Wisconsin, he was visited by members of the Nakoma Country Club. They asked him to visit their property and then commissioned him to design the clubhouse plans.

Preliminary drawings for the Clubhouse were presented to the Board of Directors near the end of 1923. Wright utilized an American Indian theme and designed the clubhouse to represent a cluster of wigwams.

In 1923, Frank Lloyd Wright designed four homes in California utilizing his textile-block

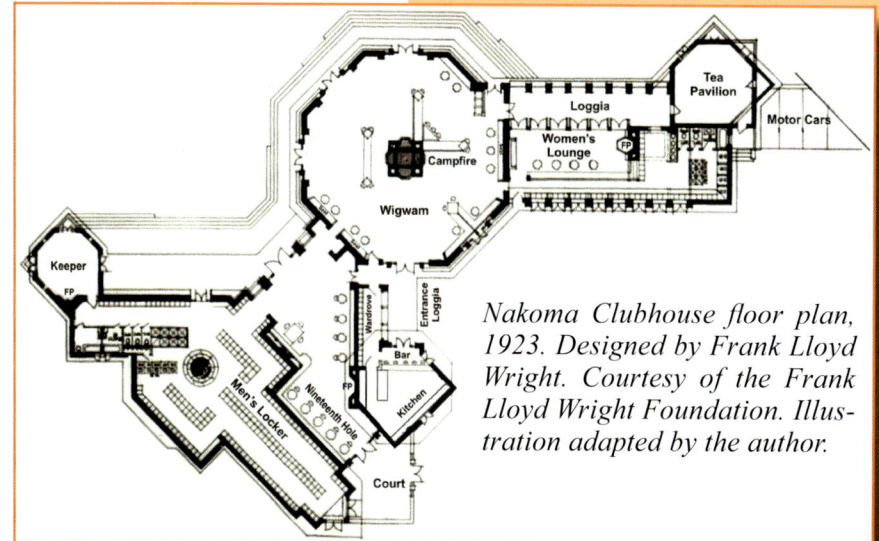

Nakoma Clubhouse floor plan, 1923. Designed by Frank Lloyd Wright. Courtesy of the Frank Lloyd Wright Foundation. Illustration adapted by the author.

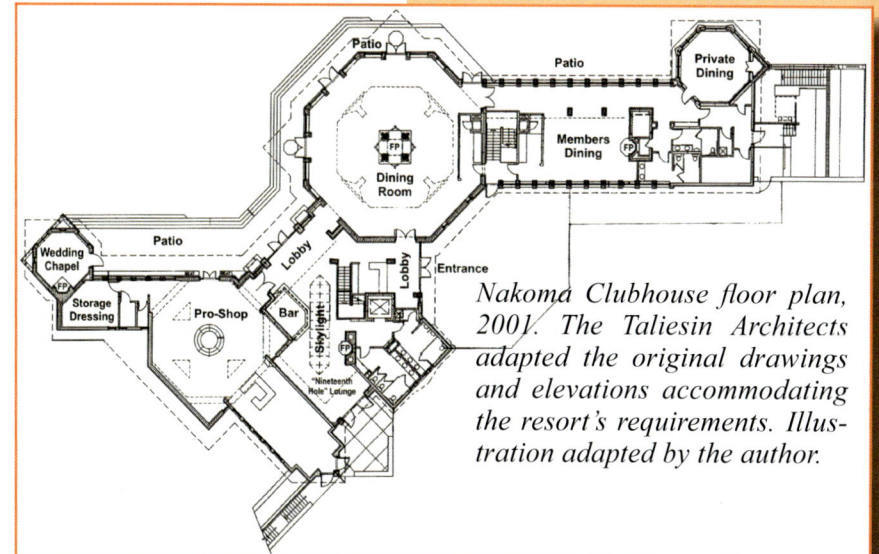

Nakoma Clubhouse floor plan, 2001. The Taliesin Architects adapted the original drawings and elevations accommodating the resort's requirements. Illustration adapted by the author.

Left: Courtesy of The Frank Lloyd Wright Foundation Archives (The Museum of Modern Art | Avery Architectural & Fine Arts Library, Columbia University, New York).

Original Drawing for the Nakoma Clubhouse,
Frank Lloyd Wright, 1923

I have never had any greater pleasure than to take a handful of colored pencils in one hand here, T square and triangle lying on a sheet of white paper, and try to feel the design of the thing I want to do. It's a great moment. — Frank Lloyd Wright, 1953

system (right). One of the options Wright presented to Nakoma utilized his textile-block system. Wright's estimated cost to complete the Clubhouse was $70,000. The initial drawings were enthusiastically embraced and Wright was given the go ahead to complete his drawings and present them to the club membership.

In August of the following year, Wright presented his drawings to the club members. The focal point of his design was a large pyramid-shaped room he labeled *"Wigwam."* At the heart of the immense room was a centrally located fireplace he labeled *"Campfire."* The plans were well received, and Wright was paid for his services, but his Nakoma Clubhouse was not built.

In 1929 the Nakoma Country Club began construction of their clubhouse designed by another architect at a significantly reduced cost. One can only speculate as to why Wright's design was rejected. It could have been the economy. As it slowed, they may have adopted a more conservative budget. Alternatively, the Nakoma Country Club may have been concerned about their public image. The Nakoma subdivision was advertised as *"an ideal place to raise a family."* From 1925 through 1928, Wright's second wife Miriam Noel mercilessly tormented and hounded him publicly. Their relationship was quite tumultuous. Coupled with Wright's financial difficulties, the family-friendly Nakoma Country Club may have wanted to avoid the adverse publicity.

Right: The John Storer Residence, one of four California textile-block homes designed by Frank Lloyd Wright in 1923. The others included the Millard (La Miniatura), Freeman and Ennis residences. The textile-block system was also utilized in the design of the Arizona Biltmore.

Drawings courtesy of The Frank Lloyd Wright Foundation Archives (The Museum of Modern Art | Avery Architectural & Fine Arts Library, Columbia University, New York).

**Original Drawing for the Memorial Gateway,
Frank Lloyd Wright, 1924**

*Memorial Gateway To Nakoma. Frank Lloyd Wright, Architect.
Nakoma "Basin." Stone memorial to Nakoma "Woman."
Nakomis "Plateau." Stone memorial to Nakomis "Warrior." FLW.*

1924: MEMORIAL GATEWAY

Although the Nakoma Memorial Gateway was related to and was to be within eyesight of the Nakoma Country Club Clubhouse, it was a separate project. When the Nakoma Subdivision was developed in 1915 by the Madison Realty Company, Paul E. Stark became the sales agent. He was on the Board of Directors for both the Nakoma County Club and, in the early 1920s, the Madison Realty Company. There were also others who were members of both boards. Wright was commissioned by the Country Club for the Clubhouse, and by the developers of the subdivision for Nakoma and Nakomis. Madison Reality took a number of steps to promote sales in the new Nakoma subdivision. They built a new school in 1917, spending $15,000, and set aside land for parks. Transportation to *"outlying"* subdivisions was lacking, so they created the first private bus line in Madison.

The Madison Realty Company determined to utilize the Nakoma theme and honor the American Indian. The Nakoma Memorial Gateway was planned for the intersection of Nakoma Road and Manitou Way.

The Memorial Gateway is only one example of Wright's appreciation of the American Indian heritage. John Lloyd Wright wrote, *"Giannini from Italy painted American Indians in brilliant colors on the walls of Papa's bedroom... Papa liked Indians!"*[2] Three American Indian murals were painted on walls in Frank Lloyd Wright's Oak Park home in 1895.

Frank Lloyd Wright's drawings for the project were comprehensive. They included birds-eye perspectives, plot plans, front, back and side views. The plan was comprised of two pools. The upper pool, *"Nakomis Plateau,"* included the 18 foot rectangular Chieftain Nakomis which Wright described as *"teaching his young son to take the bow to the Sun God."* The lower pool, *"Nakoma Basin,"* included the 16 foot circular Nakoma, which Wright described with *"brimming bowl and children, symbolic of domestic virtue."*[1] Like Wright's earlier Dana House *"Crannied Wall"* and Midway Gardens figures, both Nakoma and Nakomis were characteristically abstract and geometric in shape.

Wright's plans were well received by the Madison Realty Company. Models created by Wright were photographed on August 3, 1926. But in a letter dated August 4, 1926, the project was rejected due to the cost. Wright refused to scale down the plans, and the Gateway project was abandoned.[5]

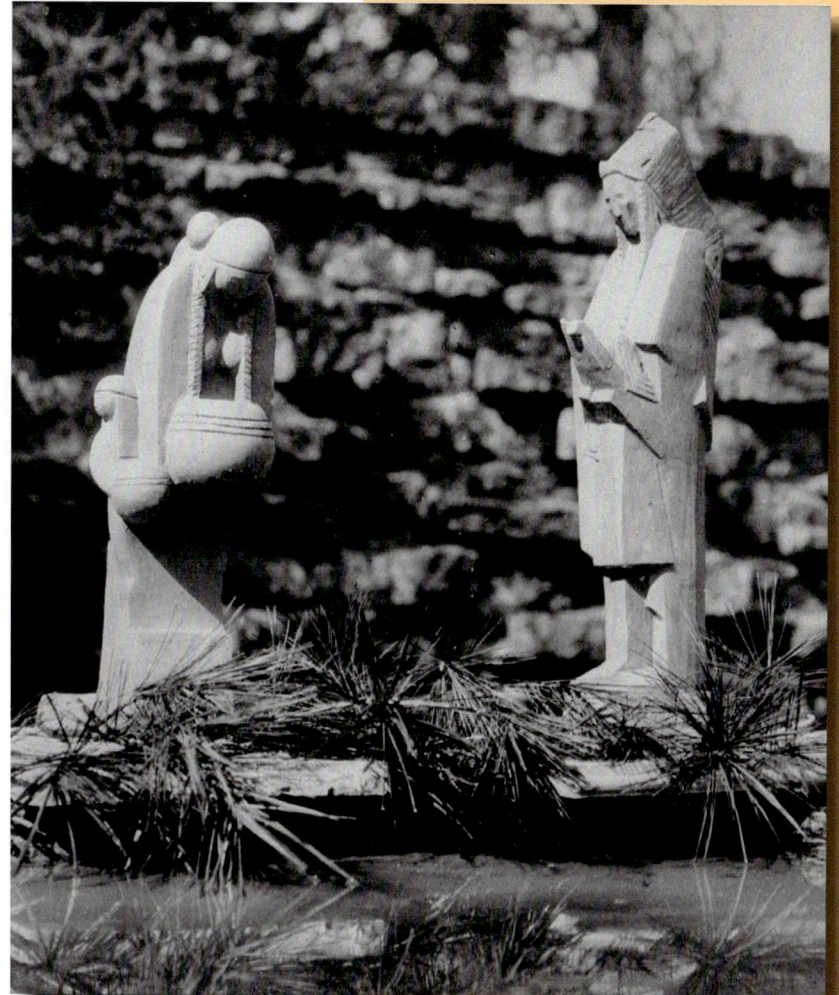

Nakoma and Nakomis models, photographed at Taliesin, Spring Green, Wisconsin on August 3, 1926 for Franz A. Aust, by Melvin E. Diemer. Courtesy of the Wisconsin Historical Society, WHS-101791.

Left: Courtesy of The Frank Lloyd Wright Foundation Archives (The Museum of Modern Art | Avery Architectural & Fine Arts Library, Columbia University, New York).

1929 Nakoma (left) and Nakomis (right) terra-cotta figures. *12.25 and 18 inches high. Each is impressed with the Frank Lloyd Wright monogram. Courtesy of Christie's, New York.*

1929: NAKOMA & NAKOMIS

Terra-cotta Nakoma and Nakomis sets were created in 1929-1930. Frank Lloyd Wright's project number for the Nakoma Sculptures was 2906, dating it as 1929. Wright's original models *(page 15)* were possibly used to create the mold for the terra-cotta sets. Of interest is Charles L. Morgan's involvement to create *"a few black sets"* of the Nakoma and Nakomis in 1930.

Not only an architect, Charles Leonard Morgan (1890-1947) had a reputation as an excellent artist. Frank Lloyd Wright was working on the National Life Insurance Company project in 1924-1925. Wright sought Morgan's help in preparing a series of perspective drawings for the project.

Due to financial difficulties, Frank Lloyd Wright was incorporated in 1927. He wrote in *An Autobiography* that *"many stories of this incorporation of myself appeared. An idea gained credence that my financial troubles were over. That I could now work with no financial harassments or restrictions..."*[6] Donald Johnson writes that Wright tried to establish a series of partnerships with architects in Chicago, New York, Phoenix and Los Angeles.[7] One of the *"Associates,"* as Wright called them, was Charles L. Morgan. Wright continued in his Autobiography, *"Charlie Morgan came forward, as a volunteer, and interested others."*

In a letter to Morgan on December 12, 1929, Wright clarified the relationship. *"I have never entered into any partnership agreement and probably never shall, being totally unfitted for that type of co-operation. I prefer 'association'..."* Wright details a fee schedule and concludes with, *"All contracts should be made and plans too, in the name of Frank Lloyd Wright, Incorporated: Charles Morgan, Chicago Associate."*[8]

Morgan was the associate architect for the Powhatan Apartments in Chicago, completed in 1929. He was responsible for the colorful mosaics in the lobbies, as well as the colorful exterior terra-cotta panels featuring scenes with Native American references. Other American Indian motifs can be found throughout the building. Of particular interest are the mosaic panels in the anteroom between the lobby and the pool. They bear a striking resemblance to the murals in the Tavern of Midway Gardens, designed by Wright in 1913. It's possible Morgan wished to honor Wright's work at the Midway Gardens, which was demolished at the same time the Powhattan Building was receiving its final touches.

During the destruction of Midway Gardens, Wright asked Morgan to assist him with an illustrated essay on Midway Gardens that was planned but

Below: 1929 Nakoma terra-cotta with black glaze. 12.25 inches high. Courtesy of Victoria & Albert Museum, London.

never published in the *Chicago Daily News.*

With the completion of the Powhatan in 1929, Wright's association in December, and American Indian motifs and terracotta molds freshly on Morgan's mind, his involvement in the Nakoma and Nakomis sets was a natural fit. In a letter to Wright dated December 23, 1930, Morgan discussed finishing the chief and squaw statues in time for Christmas, *"and after all these weeks I am having to keep at it all the time to get a few black sets..."*[9] It was possibly the same black glaze used on the Indian chiefs on the exterior of the Powhatan.

Morgan began making use of his association with Wright, signing his letters as *"Charles Morgan, Chicago Associate of Frank Lloyd Wright."* Possibly due to the Great Depression and a lack of work, Morgan traveled, giving lectures and chalktalks on modern architecture. One lecture led John Howe to become one of Wright's first apprentices in 1932.[10]

As construction began on the Wright-de-signed Annie Pfeiffer Chapel at Florida Southern College (1938), it was announced on November 26, 1938, in *The Southern,* the college paper, that *"Morgan had arrived at Florida Southern College as the personal representative of Frank Lloyd Wright."*

On April 5, 1947, Morgan was vacationing in Florida with his wife. Children playing along the shore in front of his brother's cottage accidently kicked a ball into the river. Taking a small rowboat, he attempted to retrieve it for the children, but drowned in the process. Attempts to revive him were futile.[11]

Right: The Midway Gardens Sprite, designed by Frank Lloyd Wright in 1913, was abstract and geometric in form, much like the Nakoma and Nakomis sculptures.

Top Left: Unglazed 1929 terra-cotta Nakoma, painted in gold, 12.25 inches tall. Impressed with the Frank Lloyd Wright monogram. Courtesy of Treadway Gallery, Cincinnati, Ohio.

Above: Decorative black-glazed terracotta sculpture on the exterior of the Powhatan in Chicago, designed by Charles Morgan. He indicated that he was producing a few black sets of the Wright Nakoma and Nakomis. Black may have been chosen because of the result of the black-glazed sculpture above.

1955: NAKOMA & NAKOMIS

During the early 1950s, Prince Giovanni Del Drago became an apprentice at Taliesin. His family was one of the oldest and most illustrious in Italy, primarily achieved when his grandfather married the daughter of the Queen of Spain.

Del Drago's father, Don Giovanni, immigrated to the United States in 1904 when he was 22 years old. At 27, he married Mrs. Josephine Schmid, the wealthy widow of the founder of the Lion Brewery. She was 23 years older than he was.

Giovanni Del Drago was 21 when he became a Taliesin apprentice. His interests were architecture and the arts. As an apprentice, he reproduced the Nakoma and Nakomis sculptures. *"I remember working on them in Arizona during the winter of 1955-1956 under Mr. Wright's guidance, casting them in concrete and gilding them in the studio of a sculptor in Phoenix,"* he recalled.[12]

Today the sculptures can be found at Taliesin, Spring Green.

Cast in concrete, Giovanni Del Drago finished them in gold. Nakoma (female) stands 36 inches tall. Nakomis (male) stands 44 inches tall. Courtesy of Tom Waddell.

1974 Bronze Nakoma and Nakomis.
The female Nakoma stands 12" high,
the male Nakomis stands 17.5".

1974: NAKOMA & NAKOMIS

According to Thomas Nelson Hubbard, he was given a set of Nakoma and Nakomis terra-cotta statues by his father, Willis W. Hubbard. Willis, an architect in the Chicago area, told him that he received the statues as a gift from the Otis Elevator Company.

Born in February 1931, Thomas graduated from Yale in 1953. After serving in the Army, he worked for Rand McNally & Company for nine years. He then formed his own company, Hubbard Scientific, the largest manufacturer of raised relief maps in the United States. After selling the company in 1973, he formed Crystal Productions, producing and publishing educational art and science resource materials. He was a talented watercolor artist, specializing in landscape, fly fishing and wildlife scenes.

To commemorate the fiftieth anniversary of the original design, Thomas Hubbard contacted the Frank Lloyd Wright Foundation and was granted a license to produce bronze sculptures in December 1973. Molds were created from the original terra-cotta sculptures created in 1929-30. The first bronze sets were produced by the Shidoni Foundry in Tesuque, New Mexico. The original list price was $1,650. The license specified that upon the production of 500 bronze sets, the molds would be destroyed.

Hubbard and The Frank Lloyd Wright Foundation also published the 12 page booklet *Indian Memorials*. It included a short biography of Wright,

examples of Wright's Dana House, Midway Gardens and Imperial Hotel sculptures, Wright's original drawings of the Nakoma and Nakomis, and photographs of the two new bronze sculptures.

Approximately 200 sets have been produced, and sets are still available from the Zaplin/Lampert Gallery, Sante Fe, New Mexico.

Although Thomas was involved in a hang gliding accident in 1975 that left him a paraplegic, it did not dampen his enthusiasm for life. He passed away in March 2011, at the age of nearly 80.

Left: Frank Lloyd Wright created drawings of the Nakoma and Nakomis Statues in 1924.

Right: Another Wright sculpture, "Flower in the Cranied Wall" was designed in 1902 for the Dana House, after the poem by Alfred Lord Tennyson. Richard Bock, sculptor.

Below: Indian Memorials, a twelve page booklet produced by Hubbard Associates and The Frank Lloyd Wright Foundation, 1974.

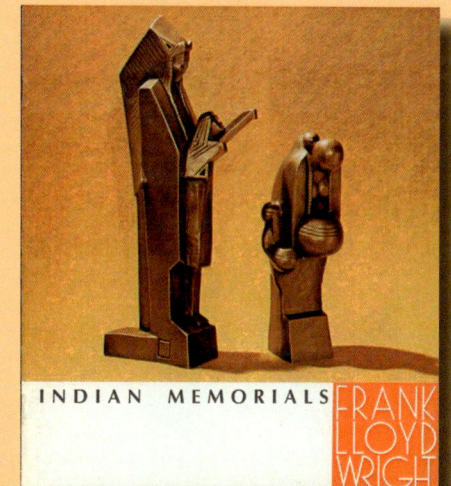

INDIAN MEMORIALS FRANK LLOYD WRIGHT

Above: Courtesy of The Frank Lloyd Wright Foundation Archives (The Museum of Modern Art | Avery Architectural & Fine Arts Library, Columbia University, New York).

© Mark Hertzberg

© Mark Hertzberg

Nakoma (left), symbolizing domestic virtue, is shown with her two children. She stands 12 feet tall and weighs 12 tons. Nakomis (right), the warrior, is depicted teaching his young son to take bow and arrow to the sun god. He stands nearly 18 feet tall and weighs nearly 40 tons. Both are made of charcoal gray Cold Spring, Minnesota granite.

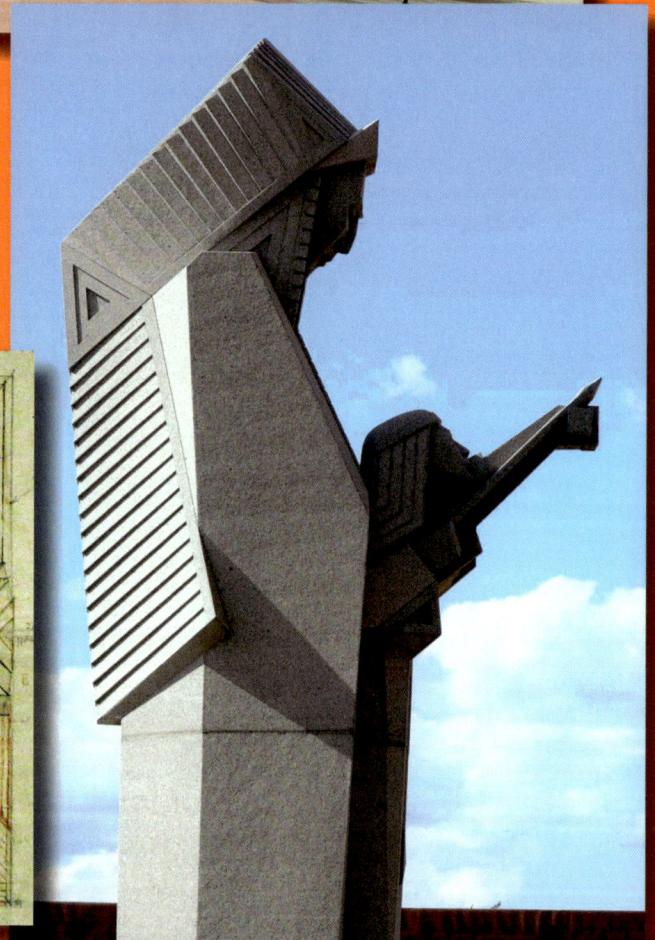

H. F. Johnson, Jr. had a desire to commemorate our nation's bicentennial by executing an unrealized Frank Lloyd Wright project. Wright designed an eight foot square plaque (right) for the SC Johnson Administration Building. It was never realized. Unable to find the original drawings, SC Johnson contacted the Frank Lloyd Wright Foundation. The unrealized Nakoma and Nakomis were suggested. After more than two years and 6,000 man hours, they were installed in 1979.

© Mark Hertzberg

Photographs courtesy of Mark Hertzberg, Racine, Wisconsin, Copyright 2013.
Illustration courtesy of The Frank Lloyd Wright Foundation Archives (The Museum of Modern Art | Avery Architectural & Fine Arts Library, Columbia University, New York).

1976: NAKOMA & NAKOMIS

In July 1936, construction was set to start on the SC Johnson global headquarters. But third generation leader H. F. Johnson, Jr. wanted a new, more modern approach. Frank Lloyd Wright was commissioned to design the company's new Administration Building in Racine, Wisconsin. Designed in 1936, the Administration Building was completed on April 22, 1939. Wright commented, *"I believe this is one of the best built buildings, technically, anywhere in the world. And I regard it not only a thoroughly modern piece of work but more nearly exemplifying the ideal of an organic architecture than any other I have built."[13]* Architects have called it the greatest contribution to business housing since the advent of the skyscraper. It is designed with rounded corners and dendriform columns. Forty-three miles of glass tubing allows soft natural light to illuminate the great room.

During the construction of the Administration Building, Johnson also commissioned Wright to design his expansive home *Wingspread* in 1937. Although apprehensive, he commissioned Wright again to design a new research and development building. The Research Tower was designed in 1944, construction began in 1947 and opening ceremonies were held on November 17, 1950.

In 1976, at the direction of H. F. Johnson, Jr., Nakoma and Nakomis sculptures were commissioned for installation on the headquarter grounds of SC Johnson. Under the direction of William Wesley Peters and Heloise Crista Swaback, they were carved by Italian sculptors Flaviano Cenderelli and Bruno Borgioli of Kotecki Monuments in Ohio. The granite was quarried in Cold Spring, Minnesota.

Edward Kotecki III recalls, *"I was very apprehensive about the project. But my father Edward Kotecki Jr. was excited with the challenge. And besides, there were no other sculptors in the county with the capability to complete such a monumental project."[14]* Life-size plaster marquettes were created by Fritz Carpenter in Racine. Each sculpture was constructed in two pieces. Once carving began, they discovered the specified granite was so hard and dense that it would be more difficult and time consuming than anticipated. It took two years and 6,000 man-hours to complete the pair of sculptures.

"Our sculptors were so skilled, that when Nakoma and Nakomis were assembled for the first time at SC Johnson's headquarters, the fit was so perfect, it needed very little modification," remembered Edward.

For the first time in more than 50 years, the full size sculptures were created as Wright had originally intended. The Nakoma sculpture is 12 feet tall and weighs 12 tons. The Nakomis sculpture is nearly 18 feet tall and weighs nearly 40 tons. Both were carved from charcoal gray Cold Spring, Minnesota granite, and adorn the courtyard of the SC Johnson Research Tower.

The sculptures were installed in 1979. *"My father, Edward Kotecki Jr., as well as our sculptors have passed,"* said Edward III. *"Creating sculptures like these are a lost art."*

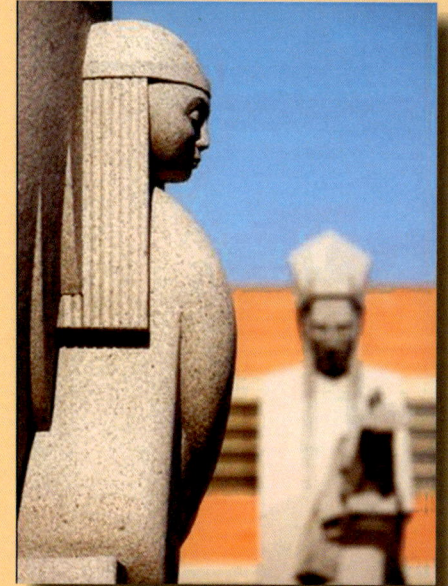

Below: In his documentary, Ken Burns considered the SC Johnson Headquarters' Great Workroom "the greatest room in the United States today."

Photographs courtesy of SC Johnson.

Nakoma Clubhouse Model, 1988.
The first three-dimensional execution of the clubhouse.

1988: CLUBHOUSE MODEL

Sixty-five years after Frank Lloyd Wright designed the Nakoma Clubhouse, a three-dimensional model was commissioned by the Elvehjem Museum of Art in Madison, Wisconsin (presently the Chazen Museum of Art). The model was constructed for the 1988 exhibition *"Frank Lloyd Wright and Madison: Eight Decades of Artistic and Social Interaction."*

Bruce Severson restored a number of existing Wright models and created two new models for the exhibition. The two new models included the Lake Mendota Boathouse — built in 1893, demolished in 1926 — and the Nakoma Clubhouse, which was designed in 1923, but never built. *"I was practicing architecture in Madison at the time, and moonlighting as a model builder,"* said Severson. *"The Museum approached me and asked if I would present a bid for the project. After winning the bid, I took a sabbatical from my practice to restore and build the models for the exhibition. I have been building models ever since.*

"Nakoma is an all wood model built at a scale of 1/8' = 1', based on plans provided by Taliesin," Severson said. *"I redrew it to the scale I was building and filled in missing information based on the drawings. The building consists of numerous sub-assemblies that are held together with hidden fasteners, a technique I used mainly to keep control of the rather complex interaction of the geometry and joinery."*[15]

The model was also included in *Frank Lloyd Wright Retrospective,* a major Japanese exhibition that took place at four different locations in 1991.

The completion of these models led Severson to other Wright projects over the years, such as the restoration of Wright's original Broadacre City for the 1995 exhibition *"Frank Lloyd Wright: Architect,"* at the Museum of Modern Art, New York.

Below: The Lake Mendota Boathouse was designed by Frank Lloyd Wright in 1893 and demolished in 1926.

Models courtesy of the Chazen Museum of Art, University of Wisconsin-Madison. Designed by Frank Lloyd Wright, fabricated by Bruce Severson.

2001: CLUBHOUSE & SCULPTURES

DARIEL AND PEGGY GARNER. In the 1970's, the Garners created a small computer software company for the banking industry. It grew from 1 office to 16 offices across the country. Tiring of the hectic schedule, they sold the company, retired and moved to a remote area of La Paz on Mexico's Baja Peninsula. There they discovered that watercress grew naturally and plentifully in the area and were soon harvesting it for distribution to Southern California stores and restaurants. Their entrepreneurial spirit blossomed into a 6,000 acre farm pioneering gourmet baby and specialty vegetables, supplying niche-market produce to North America and the rest of the world.

Upon retiring a second time in the early 1990s, they set out in search of the ideal place to build their dream home. After exploring the country, they found it in the High Sierras on Gold Mountain in Northern California. They purchased 1,280 acres, two square miles, about an hour northwest of Reno and Lake Tahoe. Unwilling to retire, plans were made for a resort, golf course and subdivision. Of the 427 building sites, 27 sold within the first month. Two-acre wooded lots started at $70,000.

The Garners contacted the Frank Lloyd Wright Foundation and began working with the Taliesin Architects in 1995. During a planning meeting they were shown the original Nakoma clubhouse plans. *"When they showed us Mr. Wright's design for Nakoma, we fell in love with it,"* said Peggy. They eventually made the clubhouse the centerpiece of the Taliesin-planned residential community.

As legend has it, while cleaning up some of the debris left on the property, Peggy picked up an old envelope that had a Frank Lloyd Wright stamp on it. That sealed their decision to build the Nakoma clubhouse.

PLANNING. In 1923, Frank Lloyd Wright presented drawings for a clubhouse to the Nakoma Country Club, which was adjacent to the Nakoma subdivision in Madison, Wisconsin. Indian symbolism could be found throughout Wright's design of the clubhouse. The Wisconsin State Journal called the Wright clubhouse *"the most unique building of its kind in America."*

Teepee spires of wood and copper rose above walls covered in stone, laid horizontally to mimic the look of natural sedimentary strata. In-

Opposite: With the dedication of 80 skilled laborers, who came to call themselves the "Nakoma Craftsmen," the clubhouse emerged from the ground in 16 months. By May, 2000, the massive skeletal framework for the dining room fireplace was set in place.

Above: In 1895, Frank Lloyd Wright commissioned Orlando Giannini to create three American Indian murals in his Oak Park Home. "Papa liked Indians," recalled John Lloyd Wright.

Left: The dining room's teepee is adorned with clerestory art glass windows and horizontal copper strips decorated with colorful ceramic beads, symbolizing those worn by the midwest American Indians.

Left: Courtesy of the Taliesin Architects.

What the American people have to learn is that architecture is the great mother art, the art behind which all the others are definitely, distinctly and inevitably related. Until the time comes that when we speak of art we immediately think of buildings, we will have no culture of our own.
— *Frank Lloyd Wright, An American Architecture, 1955: 256*

side, in signature Wright fashion, low-ceilinged entrances and hallways opened to soaring spaces. At the center of Wright's design was the octagonal *"Wigwam Room."* Exposed beams created geometric patterns. Towering ceiling walls were adorned in art glass windows and decorative abstract Indian designs. Built-in seating and custom floor coverings embellished natural flagstone flooring. Centered in the room was the *"campfire,"* a fireplace open on all four sides.

The Taliesin Architects retrieved several versions of Wright's Nakoma design from the archives. One of the Nakoma plans for the clubhouse utilized textile blocks. Wright was experimenting with concrete textile block designs in 1923 (page 13). The results were four homes built in California: Millard (La Miniatura), Storer, Freeman and Ennis residences. Another plan used stone laid in the same manner as Fallingwater (right) and Taliesin (page 31). It specified local sandstone stacked horizontally, giving the appearance of natural unquarried stone. After weighing their options, the Garners decided to execute the stone version. It had a natural, organic blend with the mountainous setting. Rose colored volcanic stone similar to native stone found on their property in the Sierra Nevadas was selected for the clubhouse.

This was not the first attempt by the Taliesin Architects to resurrect the Nakoma Clubhouse. The first was in 1967, within their design for *"The Spring Green,"* an unrealized 4,000 acre, all season resort along the Wisconsin River, for the Wisconsin River Development Corporation.[16/17]

Left: Courtesy of the Taliesin Architects.

Opposite: Beams which form the structural framing for the Pro Shop teepee will remain exposed, creating geometric patterns in the finished ceiling.

Top left: Wright gave each teepee its own unique design. The top half of the walls of the private dining room lean outward and thicken as they rise above the stone walls.

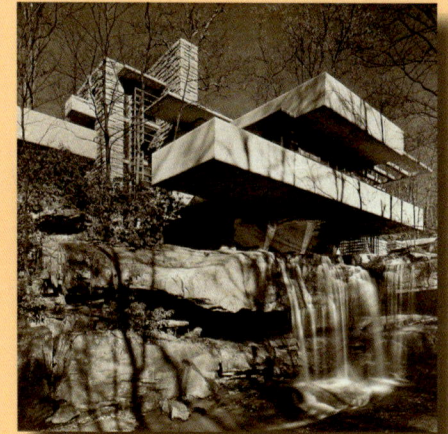

Above: Fallingwater has been considered the greatest structure ever built. Courtesy Hendrich-Blessing.

Left: By taking two squares and rotating one at 45 degrees, Frank Lloyd Wright created a continual Native American chevron pattern. The top of the largest teepee reaches the height of a six story building.

*Nakoma looks so at home with the pine trees and
mountain setting, it's almost as if Providence decreed
that this marvelous building be created here.*
— John Rattenbury, 2013

Doors to the pro shop mimic the building's shape and open outward. Wrightian styled built-in seating on the exterior wall offers spectacular views of the golf course and the Sierra Nevada Mountains.

From the initial meeting with the Garners, it took six years to adapt the Nakoma drawings and create a full set of plans, obtain permits and construct the building, which opened in 2001. Arnold Roy, Taliesin Architects' project manager, joined Taliesin in 1952 and studied under Frank Lloyd Wright. *"Except for required code upgrades, and a reallocation of interior space,"* said Roy, *"this is the building envisioned by Mr. Wright."*[18] At its heart is the Wigwam Room, a 120-seat dining area furnished with Wright-inspired carpets and octagonal chairs upholstered in Imperial Triangles fabric, first used by Wright in the 1922 Imperial Hotel, Tokyo.

Left: Courtesy of the Taliesin Architects.

Nakoma's interior design was coordinated by another Wright protégé and longtime Taliesin architect, John Rattenbury. *"Nakoma looks so at home with the pine trees and mountain setting, it's almost as if Providence decreed that this marvelous building be created here,"* said Rattenbury.[19]

CONSTRUCTION OF THE CLUBHOUSE. With the dedication of 80 skilled laborers, who came to call themselves the *"Nakoma Craftsmen,"* the clubhouse was completed in 16 months. Finished in natural stone, red cedar, copper and decorative beading, Nakoma is laid out in a series of octagons, squares and rectangular shapes. The five spires of the 24,000 square foot, $13 million clubhouse soar skyward. The largest teepee, the wigwam, is 56 feet wide and 60 feet high.

The architects at Taliesin used the floor plan and elevations from the original drawings, but

Courtesy of the Taliesin Architects.

Opposite: A February snowstorm blankets the resort and clubhouse. As if designed for this location, the Nakoma Clubhouse blends with its surroundings. The ridges of Penman Peak are visible in the background.

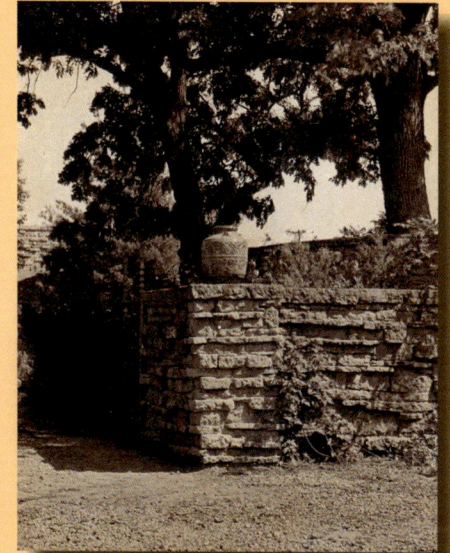

Above: Taliesin, Spring Green. View toward the garden court and Wright's residence. Stone was stacked horizontally, giving it a natural unquarried appearance. Photographed by Wright client Charles L. Manson, circa 1940.

Left: "I wanted a home where icicles by invitation might beautify the eves..."[20] Frank Lloyd Wright.

The ornamentation of a building should be constitutional, a matter of the nature of the structure beginning with the ground plan.
— Frank Lloyd Wright, "In the Cause of Architecture." Architectural Record, March 1908.

adapted the interior spaces to accommodate the resort's requirements. The original wigwam, with its built-in seating designed for gathering and relaxing, became the main dining room overlooking the golf course. It offered breathtaking views of the Sierra Nevada range. When the women's locker room was moved to the basement, the space was redesigned as the members' dining room. The adjacent Loggia, the wide open corridor, doubled as extra dining. The tea pavilion, a parlor for women, became the private dining room. A band of hand-chipped stone encircles the entire room, capping the low stone wall, creating stone windowsills.

The area originally specified as the men's locker room was also moved downstairs and redesigned as the gift and pro shop. The Nineteenth Hole Lounge remains. Secondary teepees crown each of the smaller rooms.

The clubhouse is a series of contrasting shapes and spaces. Of the five teepees the Wigwam is the most spectacular and the focus of Wright's design. Above its walls, the immense roof soars to an enclosed interior height of 40 feet above a natural flagstone floor. At the center of the dining room is the majestic stone fireplace designed with two rotated squares. The hearth opens on four sides. Surrounding the room above the walls on all eight sides is a 17-foot high, intricate Indian-motif frieze accented by giant clerestory art glass windows.

The remaining spires, wigwams and teepees are striking variations of the Indian theme. Some are decorated with hand-painted ceramic beads. Others are crowned with copper and topped with spires.

Rose-colored volcanic stone similar to the native stone found on the property would have taken years for permits and extraction. Identical rock was located in Mexico and 300 truckloads were imported. All the art glass windows and frieze work was completed on site. The interior and exterior ceramic treatments were baked in kilns built on the property.

John Rattenbury oversaw all the interior designs and details, including the dining room chairs and tables, art glass windows, custom hand-knotted carpets from China,

Opposite: The largest teepee, the Wigwam soars 60 feet high. The peak is adorned with clerestory art glass windows, mimicking the shape of the Wigwam and chimney, creating colorful patterns. Horizontal copper strips decorated with colorful ceramic beads symbolize those worn by the midwest American Indians.

Left: Built-in planters, a Wright feature, blend the Wedding Chapel with its natural surroundings.

Below: The Pro Shop peak is adorned with horizontal copper strips decorated with colorful ceramic beads that intersect with vertical copper bands. Clerestory art glass windows mimic the shape of the teepee.

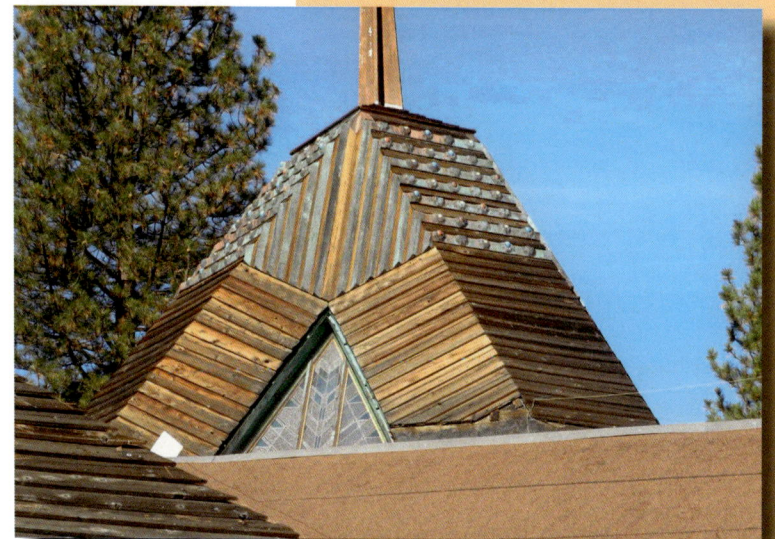

Shadows were the brushwork of the ancient architect. Let the modern now work with light, light diffused, light reflected, light refracted — light for its own sake.
— Frank Lloyd Wright, Modern Architecture, 1931: 38

even the dining room place settings. He followed the details from Frank Lloyd Wright's original plans whenever possible. Dedication ceremonies were held in May, 2001.

THE DRAGON GOLF COURSE. Although it would be another year before the clubhouse was completed, the Dragon Golf Course's dedication ceremony was held on May 27, 2000. The Garners wanted a tough course, which they achieved. It took three years to complete the course designed by Robin Nelson of Mill Valley, California. The name said it all: *"The Dragon."*

Reviews were outstanding. The May/June 2001 issue of *Ski Magazine* featured the Dragon, calling it a *"one-of-a-kind environmentally sensitive fire-breather... Its liberally contoured greens are very demanding,"* saying it was one of four courses

in the U.S. to visit. In Bob Highfill's article *"Slaying the Dragon,"* he said, *"The Dragon is a scenic masterpiece that will challenge any player"* (June 2001, *The Record*, Stockton, CA). It was voted an *"All Star Course"* by *Golf For Women Magazine,* the nation's most read women's golf magazine. In 2001, it was nominated for *Golf Digest's "Best New Course of the Year. The Dragon is an exceptional golf experience."* *AudiWorld* featured the resort in their November, 2001 issue.

Nakoma Trading Post, the resort's award-winning golf-and-retail shop, was voted a top 25 resort golf shop in the U.S. by *Golf World Business* magazine and *"2002 Merchandiser of the Year"* by the Northern California Golf Association, which included Pebble Beach. Nakoma Resort was also invited to become a member of the elite *"Small Luxury Hotels of the World."*

In 2003, Nakoma's Dragon Golf Course sponsored a $10,000 Pro-Am challenge. It was singled out for distinction in the July issue of *Golf Insider,* the industry's leading golf travel rating publication. Of the several courses it rated, the Dragon scored the highest. It was recognized for its high performance, quality offerings

Opposite: From the courtyard, the doors on the left, which open outward, lead from the terrace into the Nineteenth Hole Lounge. The teepee forms the Upper Room and is crowned with copper, decoratively painted wood trim and a spire.

Left: The Wigwam chimney (left), the Nineteenth Hole chimney (center) and the peak of the Upper Room teepee (right) can be seen over the top of the Pro Shop.

Below: Art glass doors, which open outward, lead from the terrace into the Nineteenth Hole Lounge.

*All the color and texture the eye has seen, all the rhythms
the ear has heard, all the grace of form the mind may grasp...
...are properties of architecture.*
— Frank Lloyd Wright, *Modern Architecture*, 1931: IBC

and unique status. In September, Nakoma was featured twice on the Golf Channel with a 30 minute special *"Golf With Style,"* earning acclaim for their varied and exquisite amenities. Jeff Shelley of *Golfweek* rated the Dragon a solid '6', which ranked it in the upper 15% of the finest courses in the U.S. *Golf for Women* magazine was so impressed with the course surroundings they ranked the Dragon among their *"Top 100 Fairways for Women"* in 2003.

In 2004, *Fairways & Greens* magazine ranked the Nakoma Resort one of the *"Top Golf Resorts of the West."* But by the end of 2004's season, cracks were appearing in the Dragon's armor. In August, the *Golf Course Industry* by-line read: *"Can golf with Wright be wrong? Oh, you betcha. You might think that the Garner's resort has everything it takes to be a huge success. So what's the problem? The golf course can be as ferocious as its name implies. While some golfers relish the challenge it presents, others find it excessively penal, and they're not likely to come back..."*

Within the first three years of play, par was never broken, even when hosting PGA professional tournaments.

THE DRAGON IS WOUNDED. By December 2004, the Garners ceased making payments on their loans. By October of 2005, Mr. Garner relinquished his equity interest to Ms. Garner, making her the resort's controlling member. She failed to find other investors and the resort went into bankruptcy. In April, 2006 the resort and golf course went up for auction. It was announced in the local paper that the 880 acre property had been purchased at the bankruptcy auction. The sale fell through, hopes were dashed, and the resort closed in 2006.

The resort reopened in 2008, operating while in Chapter 7, and attempted to find a buyer. Gone were the $149 green fees, free bottles of water and engraved bag tags.

Opposite: The largest teepee, the Wigwam Dining Room soars 60 feet in the air. The peak is adorned with art glass and horizontal copper strips decorated with colorful ceramic beads, symbolizing those worn by the Midwest American Indians. The art glass windows mimic the shape of the wigwam and chimney.

Top left: The fascia is coated with copper paint, speckled with a light blue-green finish, creating a patina-like effect. Art glass windows mixed with decoratively painted wood trim fill the peak of the upper room. Wright's use of piano hinges allow the inverted triangle window, hinged at the top, to swing out at the bottom.

Left: Wright turned the end of the Pro Shop 45 degrees, forming a "V." This allowed two doors to open outward. This art glass door leads from the Courtyard into the Pro Shop.

In Architecture, expressive changes of surface, emphasis of line and especially textures of material, may go to make facts eloquent, forms more significant. Elimination, therefore, may be just as meaningless as elaboration, perhaps more often is so.
— Frank Lloyd Wright, Modern Architecture, 1931: 76

The demise of the Nakoma is reminiscent of Browne's Bookstore (right), designed by Wright in 1907. Francis Fisher Browne was one of Chicago's most successful literary publisher's at the turn of the century. Bookstores at the time were always placed on the ground floor and visible from main thoroughfares. Browne threw conventional wisdom out the window and placed his bookstore on the seventh floor. The concept for the interior was unique, he wanted the feel of a living room, complete with a fireplace. Like the overwhelming praise Nakoma received, Browne's was praised as one of the premier bookstores *on this side of the water.*[21]

In hindsight, Browne should have stayed with conventional wisdom. Even with Frank Lloyd Wright's design and Browne's leadership, the bookstore struggled to run profitably. Four years after opening it was announced that *"Browne's Bookstore will remove to commodious quarters on the street floor... and by this move will take its place among the many high-class shops which line this exclusive thoroughfare. Browne's Bookstore has been known as one of the most artistically arranged bookstores in the country..."*[22] In the end, the move did not help. In April 1912 the directors decided to close the bookstore.

Whether it was the bite of the Dragon, or unrealistic expectations which brought about Nakoma's demise, it was not for lack of trying.

THE DRAGON IS TAMED. The Dragon picked off potential buyers one by one. After nearly six years in bankruptcy, it was announced in April, 2010 that the Nakoma Resort and Golf Course had been purchased by the Schomac Group, Inc.

The new owners prepared for a July reopening. They refurbished the course, seven miles of cart paths, the clubhouse and luxurious villas. Robin Nelson, the course's renowned architect, toured the course providing input for retaining its challenge, while taming the Dragon. Their goal was to soften the course, making it friendlier to a wider field of players. One thing that remained constant were the breathtaking views of the Sierra Nevada range.

Opposite: Wright gave each teepee to its own unique design. From the rows of beads, to the roof overhang, to the shape of the roof and windows, Wright's use of the Native American Indian chevron symbol is awe-inspiring. The top half of the walls of the Private Dining Room lean outward and thicken as they rise from the stone base.

Below: Browne's Bookstore, designed by Frank Lloyd Wright in 1907.

Left: "Go to Nature, consider her ways. Let your home appear to grow easily from its site, and shape it to sympathize with its surroundings if Nature is manifest there." Frank Lloyd Wright, "Art in the Home." Arts for America, June, 1898: 586.

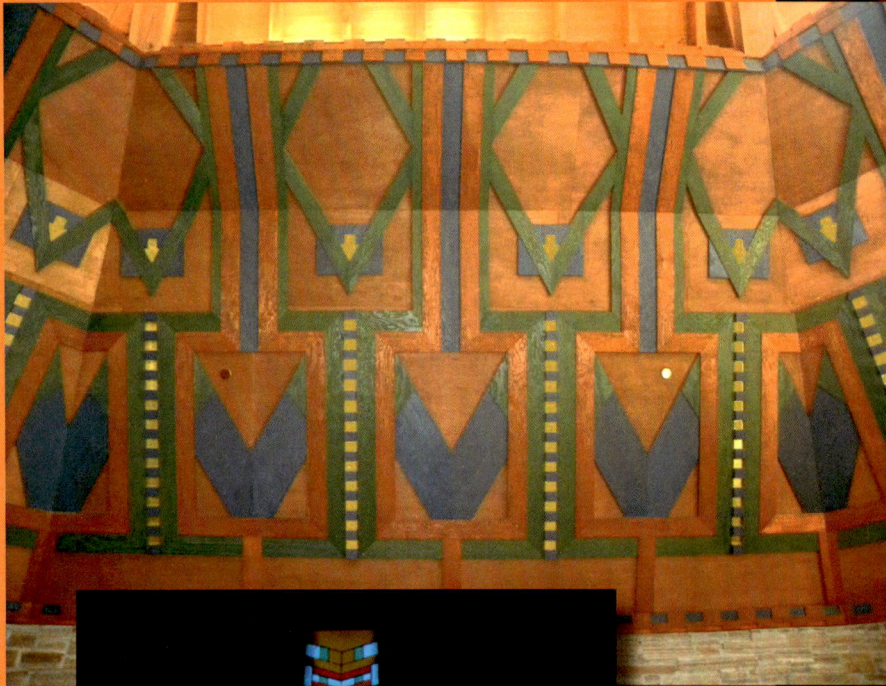

At the center of Wright's design is the octagonal "Wigwam Room" and the majestic stone "Campfire" incorporating two rotated squares. Surrounding the room above the walls on all eight sides of the interior is a 17-foot high intricate Indian-motif frieze accented by art glass clerestory windows. Exposed beams create geometric patterns.

Photo Mary E. Nichols, Courtesy Architectural Digest

2012: NAKOMA CLUBHOUSE

Frank Lloyd Wright's ability to blend building with nature is not lost with his design of the Nakoma Clubhouse. As you approach, the Clubhouse blends, flows and grows from its site. After Wright presented his drawings for the clubhouse to the Nakoma Country Club members, Madison, Wisconsin, the *Wisconsin State Journal* called the clubhouse *"the most unique building of its kind in America."* Ninety years later, those words are prophetic.

The original Nakoma subdivision, now part of Madison, was created in 1915. Developers gave it a theme honoring Native Americans. Nakoma is a Chippewa word meaning *"I do as I promise."* Driving through the neighborhood would reveal streets named Chippewa, Hiawatha, Cherokee, Ottawa, Seneca, Yuma, Council Crest and Nakoma. Community meetings were called *"councils."* Women's groups set up *"tribes."* As sales increased, the Nakoma Country Club was established on land adjacent to the subdivision.

Wright chose to embrace the American Indian theme and designed the Clubhouse to represent a cluster of wigwams. The focal point of his design was a large teepee shaped room he named *"Wigwam."* At the heart of this immense room was a centrally located fireplace he labeled *"Campfire."*

Native American symbols are prevalent in every aspect of the design. When taken as a whole, it dazzles the eye. Besides the many teepee shapes, of which there are five, other Native American symbols are prevalent. Early Native Americans would create patterns using the "chevron," an inverted "V," connecting them end to end. This pattern is present in many details of the Nakoma Clubhouse. Wright also added horizontal bands of copper to the teepees. They were decorated with colorful ceramic beads symbolizing those worn by the Native American Indians.

Many of Wright's design features are prevalent in the Clubhouse. Rose-colored volcanic stone, similar to the native stone found on the property, was imported from Mexico and stacked horizontally, giving the appearance of natural unquarried stone.

Courtesy of The Library of Congress.

Above: Aline Barnsdall Residence, "Hollyhock House." This intricately designed living room fireplace, designed in 1917, is an example of another wall design by Frank Lloyd Wright.

Left: Wright was a master at sculpting a simple sheet of wood. The color scheme includes blue, green, gold and natural wood.

Your fireplace no longer need be an inconsequential piece of wooden furniture, planked against a blank wall, with about as inviting an aspect as the coal hod or a pair of tongs, and quite as deciduous in character, but may be a substantial thing of beauty that you feel is solidly incorporated in your building.
— Frank Lloyd Wright, "Art in the Home." Arts for America, June, 1898: 585

style. The fascia is coated with copper paint, speckled with a light blue-green finish, creating a patina-like effect. Central to many of Wright's homes was the massive fireplace, giving warmth and gathering the family. Wright placed massive fireplaces in the center of the Wigwam and members' dining rooms. Fireplaces are also in the Nineteenth Hole Lounge and wedding chapel.

Wright turned the end of the pro shop 45 degrees, forming a "V." This allowed two doors to open outward. Wright gave each teepee its own unique design. The terrace doors of the pro shop mimic its teepee shape and open outward. Wrightian styled built-in seating on the exterior wall offers spectacular views of the golf course and Sierra Nevada Mountains. Clerestory art glass windows mimic the shape of the pro shop teepee.

Above: Not only do the light fixtures repeat the octagonal shape of the Wigwam dining room, they also mimic the trusses.

Top left: The Loggia offers spectacular views of the golf course and Sierra Nevada Mountains. Horizontal bands of windows accented with vertical columns dominated many of Frank Lloyd Wright's prairie-styled homes of the early twentieth century.

It was laid in the same manner as Taliesin (page 31). The largest teepee, the Wigwam reaches a height of 60 feet above ground level. The peak is adorned with art glass and horizontal copper strips, decorated with colorful ceramic beads. The clerestory art glass windows mimic the shape of the wigwam and chimney. Doors open outward to the terrace in typical Wright

Opposite: Warm rich earth tones of natural wood and stone are accented with hidden lighting. Lowered ceilings in the Loggia, enhance the 16 foot vaulted ceiling in the members' dining room. Central to many of Wright's homes was the enormous fireplace, giving warmth and gathering the family. Wright stays true to his philosophy and centralizes the fireplace in the members' dining room.

Left: This intricate wooden frieze is repeated on both sides of the members' dining room. The color scheme includes blue, green, gold and natural wood. Not only does it weave the chevron symbol into the design, but also repeats the shape of the clerestory art glass windows of the Wigwam dining room, which mimics the exterior shape of the wigwam and chimney.

WIGWAM DINING ROOM. Entering the dining room is an exhilarating and inspiring experience. At the center of Wright's design is the octagonal *"Wigwam Room."* Above its walls, the massive roof reaches an enclosed interior height of 40 feet above a natural flagstone floor. At the center of the dining room is the majestic stone *"Campfire"* incorporating two rotated squares. The hearth opens on all four sides.

Surrounding the room above stone walls on all eight sides of the interior is a 17-foot high intricate Indian-motif frieze. The color scheme includes blue, green, gold and natural wood. It is accented by giant clerestory art glass windows.

Wright was a master at sculpting a simple sheet of plywood. In 1937 Wright designed an elaborate plywood mural for the office of Edgar Kaufmann of Fallingwater. It was dismantled in 1955, and given to the Victoria and Albert Museum, London in 1973. Other wall designs include Midway Gardens (1913), the Imperial Hotel (1915) and homes like the Coonley Residence (1907) and Hollyhock House (1917).

The exposed beams create geometric patterns and bring to mind the drafting room truss structure at Taliesin. The craftsman were so skilled, it is hard to believe that the beams are not solid wood but steel beams encased in wood.

The immense clerestory art glass windows mimic the shape of the wigwam and chimney. They are nearly 10 feet wide and are 13 feet tall. The 7.5 foot high stone walls are dwarfed by the immensity of the wigwam.

MEMBERS' DINING ROOM. Originally designed as the women's wing with a lounge and tea room, Taliesin Architects redesigned the space as the members' and private dining rooms. The loggia (corridor open on one side) offers spectacular views of the golf course and Sierra Nevada Mountains. Like many of Wright's prairie styled homes of the early twentieth century, horizontal bands of windows are accented with vertical columns.

Opposite: Ceiling beams weave a pattern above the pro shop, forming one of five wigwams. Clerestory art glass windows mimic the shape of the wigwam and are 9' 2" wide and tall.

Top left: Pro shop doors open out to the terrace and spectacular views of the golf course and Sierra Nevada Mountains. Frank Lloyd Wright did not hesitate taking liberty with the design of an ordinary door, creating a unique shape in the process.

Below: Detail of the pro shop's clerestory art glass shows the intricacy of the design.

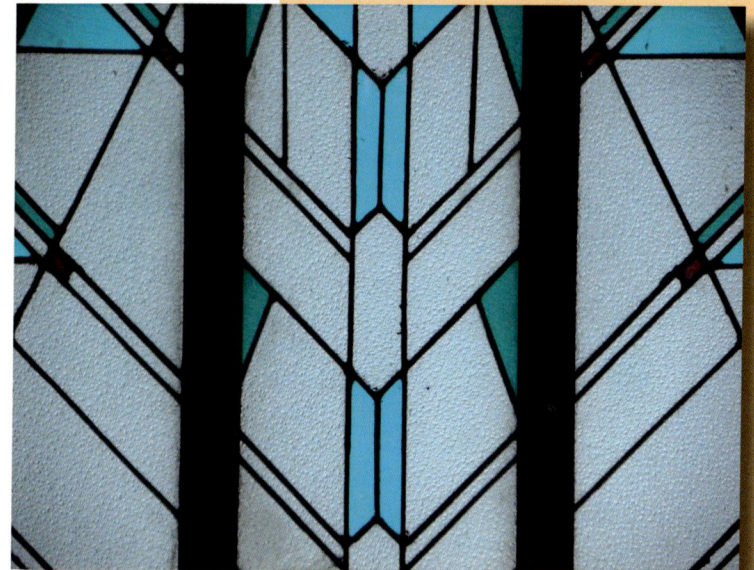

What we need today is that art shall have a new direction and artists consider the possibilities of an easy chair or the fireplace quite as important as the house itself or the picture on its walls, to the end that everything may contribute to easy utility and quiet beauty to the end, for it is not in itself that a thing is chiefly beautiful but in its relationships.
— Frank Lloyd Wright, "Art in the Home." Arts for America, June, 1898: 581

ceiling in the dining room. Central to many of Wright's homes was the enormous fireplace, giving warmth and gathering the family. Wright centralized the fireplace in the members' dining room.

Wright repeated the octagonal shape of the Wigwam dining room in the cantilevered stone fireplace, dining room chairs and the hanging light fixtures in the members' dining room.

An intricate wooden frieze is repeated on both sides of the members' dining room and to the right of the fireplace. The color scheme includes blue, green, gold and natural wood. Not only did Wright weave the chevron symbol into the design, but he repeats the shape of the clerestory art glass windows of the Wigwam dining room, which mimics the exterior shape of the wigwam and chimney. Squares hang like symbolic gold beads, reminiscent of Midway Gardens and the Imperial Hotel.

Broad overhangs block direct sunlight, allowing soft natural light to flood the members' dining room. Raised windows offer a measure of privacy.

PRIVATE DINING ROOM. Originally designed as a women's tea room, it takes the same footprint as the larger Wigwam dining room. Windows form three sides of an octagon. A band of hand-chipped stone encircles the entire room, capping the low stone wall and creating stone windowsills.

The two panels on either side of the door are repeated on the interior windows. The art glass design incorporates the chevron symbol and flows from panel to panel. Invert the doors, and five wigwams of different heights begin to immerge.

NINETEENTH HOLE LOUNGE. Tucked next to the elevator is a unique doorway. The interior angle of an octagon is 135 degrees, and so is the angle of the door that opens to a spiral staircase and leads to the upper room, the only second level at the Nakoma Clubhouse.

Art glass doors lead from the Nineteenth Hole Lounge to an enclosed terrace. Custom barrel chairs and coffee tables were designed by the Taliesin Architects. The massive 6 by 30 foot overhead art glass skylight is stunning. Rattenbury

Above: Private dining doom. The art glass design flows from panel to panel. Invert the doors, and wigwams of different heights begin to emerge, five in all.

Left: Tucked next to the elevator is a unique doorway. The interior angle of an octagon is 135 degrees, and so is the angle of this door. It opens to a spiral staircase which leads to the upper room.

Opposite: Art glass doors lead from the Nineteenth Hole Lounge to an enclosed terrace. Custom barrel chairs, coffee tables and carpets were designed by the Taliesin Architects. Rattenbury oversaw all the interior designs and details, following details from Wright's original plans whenever possible.

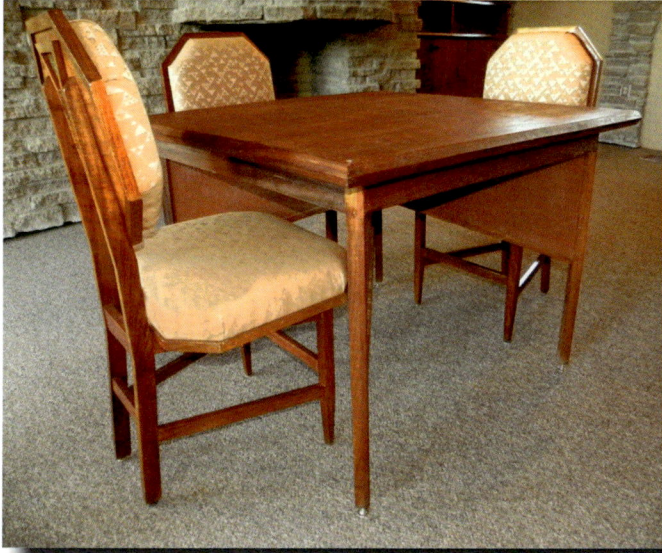

FURNITURE. Frank Lloyd Wright designed over 1,100 pieces of furniture in his lifetime. He first designed the barrel chair for the Darwin Martin Residence (1904). In 1905, he designed a barrel chair for the Frank L. Smith Bank. Slight modifications were made to the Martin design for the H. F. Johnson Jr. Residence, Wingspread (1937). He liked the design so much that when the order was placed for Johnson, he ordered a dozen for Taliesin. The design of the Nakoma barrel chairs utilizes five sides of the octagon. Nakoma chairs are upholstered with fabric by Schumacher. *"Imperial Triangle"* can be seen throughout the clubhouse in teal, beige and ivory colors, and was first manufactured in 1986. It is reminiscent of *"Design No. 705,"* Schumacher/Wright, 1955.[23]

Built-in seating, another Wright trademark,

oversaw all the interior designs, following details from Wright's original plans whenever possible.

PRO SHOP. Doors on the north side of the pro shop open to the terrace and spectacular views of the golf course and Sierra Nevada Mountains. Wright did not hesitate to take liberty with an ordinary door, creating a unique design in the process.

Ceiling beams weave a pattern above the pro shop, forming one of five wigwams. Although not as tall as the Wigwam dining room, it reaches a height of 36 feet, 56 when adding its spire. The clerestory art glass windows mimic the shape of the wigwam and are 9' 2" tall and wide. The art glass design is reminiscent of the Ennis Residence designed in 1923.

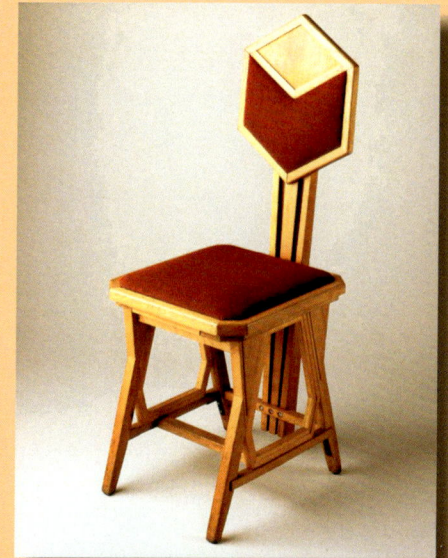

Above: Wright designed over 1,100 pieces of furniture in his lifetime. One example is the Imperial Hotel "Peacock" side chair, designed between 1916-1922.

Below: Chairs repeat the octagon footprint of the wigwam. The shape of the wigwam clerestory art glass windows is inverted and incorporated into the design on the back of the chairs.

Color has a significance all its own, and is in a realm all its own. Color is the music of light, you see.
— Frank Lloyd Wright, Photography, February 1954: 118

can be seen in the lounge. Stories abound of Frank Lloyd Wright visiting homes he designed, rearranging furniture as he had originally intended it. Built-ins assured their placement.

The Nakoma dining room table legs are not just legs, but a design that masters space. Coffee tables are a reduced version of this design.

TREASURES ABOUND.

Wright, an expert in Japanese prints, was fond of collecting Asian art. Hidden in plain view *(right)*, in a corner, at the far end of the pro shop is an elaborate, ornate Chinese carving reaching to a height of over seven feet.

A painting by Alexander Dzigurski II can be found in the pro shop: *"Saturday Afternoon Picnic with the Wrights."* Mr. Dzigurski met the Garners when they moved to California in the early 90s. He was contacted by Dariel Garner in 2000 and commissioned to create a painting of Wright for the Nakoma Clubhouse dedication ceremony in May 2001. They provided Mr. Dzigurski with a dozen photographs, adapting Wright's afternoon picnics, and incorporating the Sierra Nevada Mountains in the background.[24]

THE GOLD MOUNTAIN COMMUNITY.

When the Garners subdivided their property, they wove 427 building sites throughout the 18 hole golf course creating an environmentally sensitive, gated, golf and recreational community. Community guidelines mandated non-reflective building materials and a palette in harmony with nature. Fencing and lawns were not permitted, retaining a natural look. At least two materials were required to be used on each side of the exterior.

Some homes were designed with acid-aged copper trim in Frank Lloyd Wright inspired patterns. By 2002, 40 homes had been designed by Taliesin architects. Half were adapted from a handful of standardized plans, which were supplied to buyers at no charge.

A WRIGHT MASTERPIECE.

Although the Clubhouse is more than ten years old, it has not lost its luster as a Wright masterpiece, and continues to excite Wright enthusiasts who come to experience what the *Wisconsin State Journal* heralded in 1924 as *"the most unique building of its kind in America."* The Nakoma Clubhouse truly is a Wright Masterpiece. It is not difficult to imagine Wright blessing the Nakoma Clubhouse with his signature red ceramic tile.

Above: *"Saturday Afternoon Picnic with the Wrights,"* oil on canvas, Alexander Dzigurski II, 2001, 50 x 50. It is after a photograph by Pedro E. Guerrero, Taliesin, Spring Green, Wisconsin, 1940. *"On one Saturday in 1940, the entire fellowship and some guests gathered on the hill below Taliesin to enjoy the summer's bounty,"*[25] Pedro E. Guerrero.

Left: Courtesy of the Nakoma Golf Resort.

NAKOMA GOLF: THE DRAGON

Perched above the wild and scenic Feather River in northern California's Plumas County, the Dragon Golf Course is a true mountain course with stunning views from every tee box.

From its inception, reviews were outstanding. The Dragon was voted an *"All Star"* course by *Golf For Women Magazine*. It was nominated for *Golf Digest's "Best New Course of the Year."* AudiWorld featured the Resort in the November 2001 issue. It was singled out for distinction in *The Golf Insider*, the industry's leading golf-travel-rating publication. Of the several courses it rated, the Dragon scored the highest. *Golfweek* ranked the Dragon in the upper 15% of the finest courses in the U.S. *Golf for*

Opposite: Hole #1 - Dragon's Lookout. Tees are perched high above the fairway, offering a spectacular view of Eureka Peak.

Below: Hole #5 - Hope. The first of four par 3s. Sit back and enjoy a true par 3 mountain experience.

Photographs courtesy of the Nakoma Golf Resort.

Women magazine was so impressed with the course surroundings that it ranks the Dragon among its *"Top 100 Fairways for Women."* In 2004, *Fairways & Greens* magazine ranked the Nakoma Resort one of the *"Top Golf Resorts of the West."* But the Dragon had a bite.

In April, 2010, the Nakoma Resort and Golf Course was purchased by the Schomac Group, Inc.

They immediately set out preparing for a July 2010 reopening. Robin Nelson, the course's renowned architect, toured the course providing input for retaining its challenge, while taming the Dragon. Their goal was to soften the course, making it friendlier to a wider field of players. One thing that remained constant were the breathtaking views of the Sierra Nevada range.

Opposite: Hole #13 - Defiance. The longest of the par 3s offers a true mountain course feel.

Below: Hole #17 - Dragon's Pearl. The last of the Dragon par 3s is one of its finest gems. A large two-tier green ensures an exciting close to a memorable round.

Photographs courtesy of the Nakoma Golf Resort.

"The villas were designed with a sense of adventure," said Newland. *"Step through the front door and the open living spaces give a sense that they go on and on. As you work your way toward the patios, the nooks and crannies create all kinds of possibilities."*[27]

NAKOMA GOLF RESORT VILLAS

Elisabeth Winnen was a student at the Frank Lloyd Wright School of Architecture in 1995. *"I overheard Arnold Roy discussing the project with Dariel and Peggy Garner, and it piqued my interest,"* said Winnen. *"I asked Arnold if I could be involved in the project."*[26] She was soon working on the master plan and hiking the property with Arnold and the Garners, searching for the best placement of the clubhouse.

It was at the School of Architecture that she met her husband, Martin Newland. A year after they both graduated, they received a phone call from the Garners and were offered the opportunity to develop the master plan for the Villas. Martin and Elisabeth quit their jobs and moved to Gold Mountain. The master plan for the Villas encompassed 40 acres and included 70 villas.[27]

Of the four Wright inspired Villa designs, three were utilized. The Mountain is a one story, one bedroom, 775 square foot villa. The Tower is a two story, one bedroom, 964 square foot villa. The largest is the Butterfly, a one story, two bedroom 1,120 square foot villa. The first 12 Villas have been completed and are located along the 10th fairway. They feature central stone fireplaces, spacious bathrooms, saunas and private outdoor hot tubs. With an octagonal footprint, pitched roofs and sculptural stone fireplaces, the villas pay homage to the geometric approach Wright envisioned for the Clubhouse.

As is the case in every villa, the central fireplace, a Wright hallmark, emphasizes the warmth and welcome of "hearth and home."

So successful were the Villas that the internationally famed *"Small Luxury Hotels of the World"* asked the Villas at Nakoma to join its affiliate group, becoming one of only four hotels in California.

Photographs courtesy of the Nakoma Golf Resort.

NAKOMA & NAKOMIS

NICHOLS BROTHERS STONEWORKS was involved in creating the original Nakoma and Nakomis sculptures for the Nakoma Golf Resort in Northern California.

According to D. R. Hendel of Nichols Bros., they were contacted in 2001 to create a set for the Nakoma Golf Resort. Because a full sized set already existed at the SC Johnson Headquarters in Racine, Wisconsin, this set would be created at 90% of the original height, 11 1/2 and 16 feet tall. Sculptor Ivy Nichols created full size sculptures out of plaster. Rubber molds was formed around the plaster sets. Finally concrete was poured into the molds and left to dry for two weeks before the molds were removed. Nakoma and Nakomis were transported to California and placed on pedestals that were awaiting their arrival. Once installed, the set was painted gold, much like one of the 1929-30 terra-cotta sets and the 1955 Giovanni Del Drago set.

After successfully creating and installing the set at the Resort, they obtained a license from the Frank Lloyd Wright Foundation in 2004 to produce and sell sets in two different sizes. The smaller Nakoma and Nakomis set is 24" and 36" respectively, and the larger sets are 36" and 54". Cast in reconstituted stone, the smaller set is available in cream, the larger sets in five different colors.

HF COORS COMPANY was founded in 1925 by Herman Franklin Coors, son of the renowned brewer. In 2003, it was acquired by Catalina China, Inc. of Tucson, Arizona.

Near the beginning of 2011, HF Coors was licensed by the Frank Lloyd Wright Foundation to create a dinnerware collection featuring the *"Whirling Arrow"* pattern. The license expanded to include the ceramic Nakoma and Nakomis.

Molds were created from an original 1974 Hubbard set. The size reduction is due to shrinkage during the drying process. Nakoma stands 10 1/2", and Nakomis 15 1/2". Both are slate gray.

Courtesy of the HF Coors Company.

SELECTED BIBLIOGRAPHY

Alofsin, Anthony. *Frank Lloyd Wright: An Index to the Taliesin Correspondence.* New York: Garland Publishing, 1988.

—. *Frank Lloyd Wright, The Lost Years, 1910-1922.* Chicago: The University of Chicago Press, 1998.

"Clubhouse Opens at Gold Mountain." *Frank Lloyd Wright Quarterly,* Summer, 2001: pp. 28-29.

De Fries, H. *Frank Lloyd Wright: Aus Dem Lebenswerke Eines Architekten.* Berlin: Verlag Ernst Pollak, 1926.

De Long, David D. *Frank Lloyd Wright: Designs for American Landscape 1922-1932.* New York, Harry N. Abrams, 1996.

Frank Lloyd Wright. Chicago: Kelmscott Gallery, 1981.

Frank Lloyd Wright Retrospective. Mainichi Newspapers, 1991.

Futagawa, Yukio, and Bruce Brooks Pfeiffer. *Frank Lloyd Wright Preliminary Studies 1917-1932.* Tokyo: A.D.A. Edita, 1986.

Gruber, John, Editor. "The Wright Legend in Madison." *On Wisconsin,* December, 1987.

Guerrero, Pedro E. *Pedro E. Guerrero, A Photographer's Journey.* New York: Princeton Architectural Press, 2007.

Hall, Christopher. "Nakoma. A Mountain Retreat Built around a Wrightian Dream." *Architectural Digest,* November, 2002: Offprint.

Hamilton, Mary Jane. "Wright's Nakoma Country Club: An Unrealized Madison Masterpiece." *The Journal of Historic Madison,* Volume VII, 1981-82.

—. "Frank Lloyd Wright & His Automobiles." *Frank Lloyd Wright Quarterly,* Winter, 2010: pp. 4-19.

—. *Frank Lloyd Wright and Madison: Eight Decades of Artistic and Social Interaction.* Madison: Elvehjem Musuem of Art, University of Wisconsin-Madison, 1990.

—. *Frank Lloyd Wright & The Book Arts.* Madison: Friends of the University of Wisconsin-Madison Libraries, 1993.

Harris, Neil and Teri J. Edelstein. "The Powhatan." *Chicago Art Deco Society Magazine,* Fall 05/Winter 06: pp. 13-20.

Heggland, Timothy F. *The Nakoma Neighborhood, a walking tour.* Madison: Madison Landmarks Commission and the Nakoma Neighborhood, 2002.

Hertzberg, Mark. *Frank Lloyd Wright's SC Johnson Research Tower.* San Francisco: Pomegranate, 2010.

—. *Wright In Racine. The Architect's Vision For One American City.* San Francisco: Pomegranate, 2004.

Hitchcock, Henry-Russell. *In The Nature of Materials: 1887-1941, The Buildings of Frank Lloyd Wright.* New York: Duell, Slone and Pearce, 1942.

Hoffmann, Donald. *Frank Lloyd Wright, Louis Sullivan and the Skyscraper.* Mineola, New York: Dover Publications, 1998.

Johnson, Donald Leslie. *Frank Lloyd Wright Versus America, The 1930s.* Cambridge, Mass: MIT Press, 1990.

Keland, W. H. *The Spring Green.* Spring Green, Wisconsin: The Wisconsin River Development Corp., 1968.

Lipman, Jonathan. *Frank Lloyd Wright and The Johnson Wax Building.* New York, Rizzoli, 1986.

Mollenhoff, David V. and Hamilton, Mary Jane. *Frank Lloyd Wright's Monona Terrace.* Madison: The University of Wisconsin Press, 1999.

Owings, Frank N. Jr. "The Nakomis and Nakoma Statues." *Frank Lloyd Wright Quarterly,* Fall, 2006: pp. 14-17.

Pfeiffer, Bruce Brooks. *Nakoma, Nakomis. Winnebago Indian Memorials.* Scottsdale: The Frank Lloyd Wright Foundation. Aspen, Colorado: Hubbard Associates, 1974.

—. *Frank Lloyd Wright 1917-1942.* Hohenzollernring, Germany: Taschen, 2010.

—. *Frank Lloyd Wright Preliminary Studies 1917-1932.* Tokyo: A.D.A. Edita, 1986.

—. *Letters to Architects, Frank Lloyd Wright.* Fresno: Press at California State University, 1984.

—. *Treasures of Taliesin.* Fresno: The Press at California State University. Carbondale and Edwardsville: Southern Illinois University Press, 1985.

Schumacher's Taliesin Line of Decorative Fabrics and Wallpaper, Chicago: E. W. Bredemeier & Co., 1955.

Tafel, Edgar. *About Wright.* New York: John Wiley & Sons, 1993.

Tekker, Archie. "Nakoma is Built." *Taliesin Fellows Newsletter,* October 15, 2002: p. 3.

Twombly, Robert C. *Frank Lloyd Wright, His Life, and His Architecture.* New York: John Wiley & Sons, 1979.

Wright, Frank Lloyd. *An Autobiography.* New York: Longmans, Green and Company, 1932.

—. *A Testament.* New York: Horizon Press, 1957.

Wright, John Lloyd. *My Father Who is on Earth.* New York: G. P. Putnam's Sons, 1946.

FOOTNOTES:

1. Bruce Brooks Pfeiffer, *Frank Lloyd Wright Preliminary Studies 1917-1932.* Tokyo: A.D.A. Edita, 1986, p. 109.
2. John Lloyd Wright, *My Father Who is on Earth.* (New York: G. P. Putman's Sons, 1946), p. 34.
3. Ibid., p. 18.
4. Lewis Mumford, *The Highway and the City.* New York: Hartcourt, 1963, p. 139.
5. Mary Jane Hamilton, *Frank Lloyd Wright and Madison: Eight Decades of Artistic and Social Interaction.* Madison: Elvehjem Museum of Art, 1990, p. 86.
6. Frank Lloyd Wright, *An Autobiography.* Wright, New York: Longmans, Green and Company, 1932, p. 294.
7. Donald Leslie Johnson, *Frank Lloyd Wright Versus America, The 1930s.* Cambridge: MIT Press, 1990, p. 11.
8. Bruce Brooks Pfeiffer, *Letters to Architects, Frank Lloyd Wright.* Fresno, CA: Press at California State University, 1984, pp. 79-80.
9. Charles Morgan, letter to Frank Lloyd Wright, December 23, 1930, Research Library, Getty Research Institute, Los Angeles, California.
10. Edgar Tafel, *About Wright: An Album of Recollections.* New York: John Wiley & Sons, 1993, p. 124.
11. *The Independant Newspaper,* St. Petersburg, Florida, April 7, 1947, p. 2.
12. Giovanni Del Drage, correspondence with the author, April 21, 2013.
13. Bruce Brooks Pfeiffer, *Frank Lloyd Wright Collected Writings, Volume 3, 1931-1939.* New York: Rizzoli International, 1993, p. 328.
14. Edward Kotecki III, conversations with the author, January 2013.
15. Bruce Severson, correspondence with the author, January 14, 2013.
16. Robert C. Twombly, *Frank Lloyd Wright: His Life and His Architecture.* New York: John Wiley & Sons, 1979, p. 402, 405.
17. W. H. Keland, *The Spring Green,* Spring Green, Wisconsin: The Wisconsin River Development Corp., 1968, p. 22-23.
18. Arnold Roy, conversation with the author, November 2, 2012.
19. John Rattenbury, conversation with the author, April 2, 2013.
20. Wright, Frank Lloyd. *An Autobiography.* New York: Longmans, Green and Company, 1932, p. 176
21. *Publisher's Weekly,* Aug. 26, 1911.
22. Ibid.
23. *Schumacher's Taliesin Line of Decorative Fabrics and Wallpaper,* Chicago: E. W. Bredemeier & Co., 1955, Design No. 705.
24. Alexander Dzigurski II, conversation with the author, January 30, 2013.
25. Pedro E. Guerrero, *Pedro E. Guerrero, A Photographer's Journey,* New York: Princeton Architectural Press, 2007, p. 60.
26. Elizabeth Winnen, conversation with the author, September 12, 2013.
27. Martin Newland, conversation with the author, September 10, 2013.